LAKE COMO

Villas and Gardens

The architectural treasures

Brunner & C.

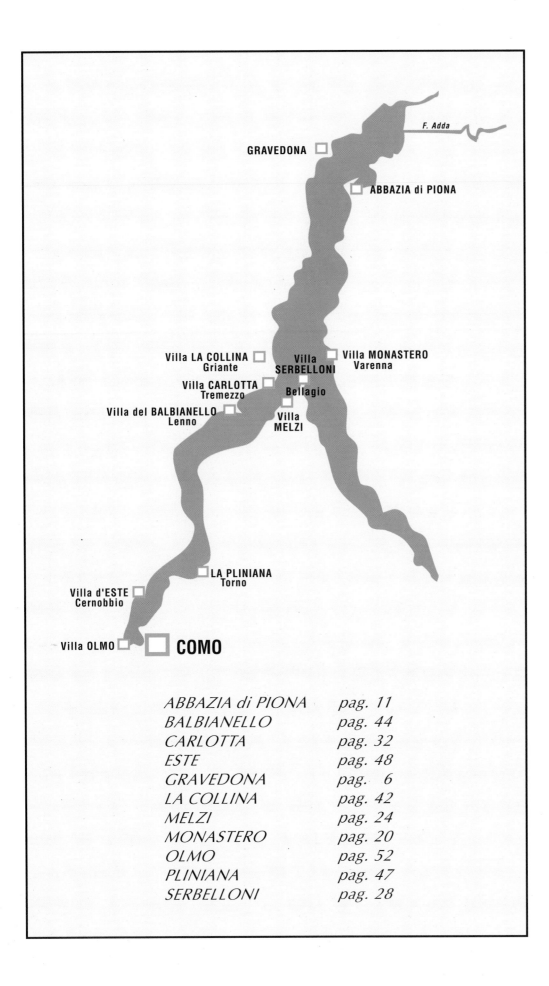

GRAVEDONA

ABBAZIA di PIONA

Villa LA COLLINA
Griante

Villa
SERBELLONI

Villa MONASTERO
Varenna

Villa CARLOTTA
Tremezzo

Bellagio

Villa del BALBIANELLO
Lenno

Villa
MELZI

F. Adda

LA PLINIANA
Torno

Villa d'ESTE
Cernobbio

Villa OLMO

COMO

Villas and Gardens

The Lake of Como,
a first encounter with the myth of the South

Even today the passage of the Alpine barrier cannot but induce an emotion of expectancy in the mind of travellers and tourists who come to Italy from Northern countries. Nowadays the mountains and the valleys are easy to cross, but the Alpine range still represents a line of demarcation which, as it did in the days of old, divides not just two different geographical worlds but, perhaps, also two different ways of life.

Up in the cold countries of the North, the grey atmosphere of incessant and monotonous work of production is made more harsh by a tradition of ethical rigidity which is ever watchful over periods of rest and free time. The South on the other hand is the land where "the lemon grows", a land where hopes will be fulfilled. Here, among the many problems which beset modern life, satisfaction is provided to those who subordinate their unceasing search for happiness and serenity under a brighter sun and a more colourful sky. In this atmoshere literary and historical ideas and memories blend with the richness of the vegetation, with the beauty of the landscape, with the pure taste of the wine, with the spontaneous nature of song, and with human contact which is so important a feature of the outgoing disposition of the local inhabitants. These are the essential ingredients, partly real, partly imagined, of what is called the "joy of living". All will seek to find it, perhaps too hopefully, in this Country, Italy, which, in the European mind, is still the preserve of great art, of love, of the "dolce far niente", where ambivalence appears to allow to every human being a degree of detachment from over - strict and restraining obligations.

It is certainly more difficult for the tourist of today to allow himself a protracted and exhaustive stay, of the kind that was possible for Goethe and Heine, Stendhal and Taine, Robert Browning and Tchaikovski, but the «Italian Tour» still retains its mythical quality for those who cross the Alps and reach the area of the Lakes of Lombardy. This myth of the South suddenly becomes visible and real. Even the innermost expectations, fanned by ancient descriptions and innumerable travel brochures, seem to take shape, and an opportunity is offered for all hopes to be fulfilled.

In Spring, reaching the shore of the Lake of Como, and just having passed through the crags and the winds of the Gothard, the tourist finds himself unexpectedly immersed in what appears to be a peremptory summons to the Mediterranean, a call which Nature has decided to insert between the harsh unwelcoming glaciers and flat and fertile plains. This is obviously a mild and restrained foretaste of the climatic explosion which will hit the traveller from the North intending to preceed to the Mediterranean South. It will also be perhaps a final summary of the principal experiences which he will have had, upon his return home.

The immigrant Greeks of the first century B.C. must have experienced the same sense of surprise when they travelled North up the peninsula. In a land so different from the one they had just left they discovered the shores of the Lario and in these they recognized unhoped-for similarities to their own maritime shores. Here they settled and transplanted their olive trees, and here they left a memory of their own villages by giving their settlements familiar sweet sounding names by which many centres of the Lake are still known: Lenno, Nesso, Lenma...

Perhaps this was the first, ancient, impact of culture known to us, since we know little (or specialists alone know) of the Neolithic settlements of the Celts, the Insubres, the Early Comenses, the Etruscans and the Gauls, races which suceeded each other, intermingled and settled upon the shores of the Lake of Como.

And with much greater difficulty would we be able to trace the tremendous activity of the Adda glacier which melted in the Quaternary period, and excavated the branches of the Lario between the mountains.

This is today an almost incredible view when observed from the spur of Bellagio, where the three branches of the Lario can be seen to meet. From this most beautiful spot one can see, on the horizon to the North a mountain range lightly covered with snow, and the rocky mass of the Grigna. One can thus visualize the inhospitable cold and the fierce geological violence, a picture which the natural structures of Spring quickly dispel, using all the devices of the season, sometimes even to excess, so that the view sometimes appears as overdone as a picture calendar. There are hedges of flowers of deep colours, breezes sometimes so scented as to suggest the descriptive writings of Tasso and Marino: often rendered more poignant by sudden gusts of oleander and jasmine which strike one as the strains of an Andante by Mozart.

Nature has certainly provided the essential elements of the scenario, but cultivation, the work of man and his imaginative inventiveness, has later transformed it into various parts and each of these has imparted a significance forever changing to the general atmosphere of the Lake.

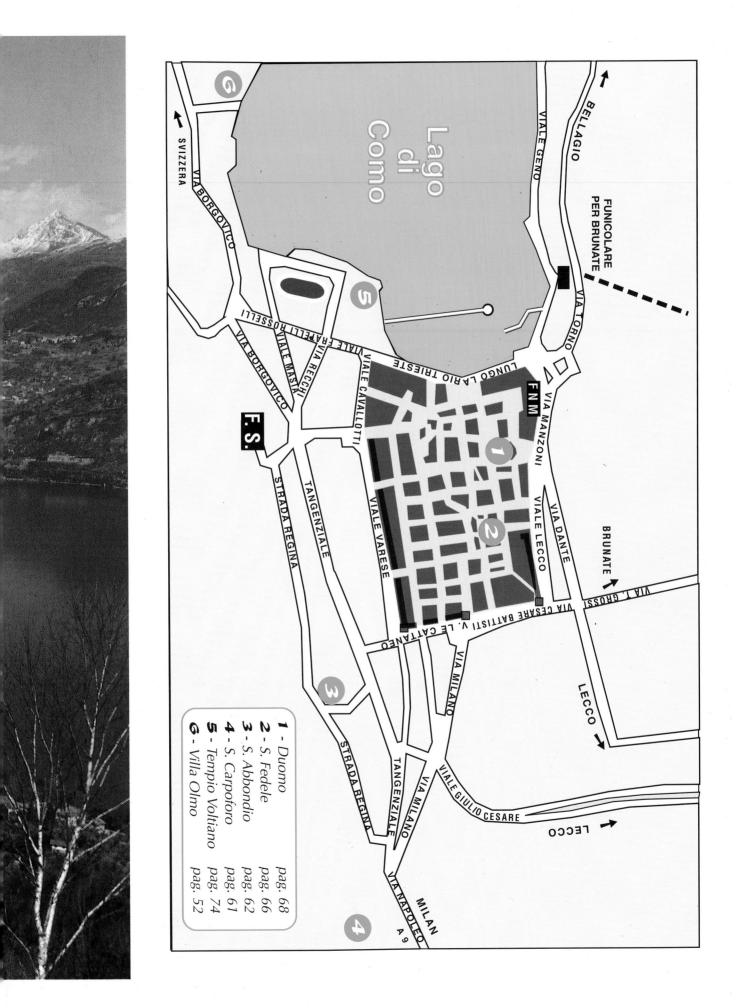

Lago di Como

FUNICOLARE PER BRUNATE

The architectural treasures

The Lake as a romantic invention

We refer, of course, to the nineteenth century. It was, in fact, the romantic period which, as it were, invented the Lake: yet another myth of nature, the character of serenity and civilized landscape placed alongside the already established concepts of the "immaculate and inaccesible heights", and the immense and stormy ocean.

Life on the Lario was obviously enjoyed even in ancient times, but the references and recollections of it which we read, for instance, in the letters of Pliny, a native of Como, in the Roman era, sound more like the profession of his love for his home town (as indeed do those of Catullus dedicated to this own Benaco), rather than a true reflection of the particular and complex fascination of the Lake as such. A geographical and psychological entity was discovered only in a period of timorous sensitivity, after the relation of man and nature had undergone a new way of thinking. This subordinated the physical perception of the world to the mood of him who contemplates it.

Thus, in the romantic period, the Lake ceased to be considered merely a basin suitable for navigation and fishing. Its shores were no longer thought of as convenient and sunny shelters which favoured the cultivation of vegetation elsewhere impossible at this latitude, of the olive and the vine. The Lakes became "places of the mind", more intimate and comprehensible than the sea, within their limited boundaries. They were seen as shimmering expanses of water, charming though melancholy, small beaches and little ports, inlets and headlands, small islands and a thousand other features of the landscape. Even in their infinite variety, they were changeable by the hour and by the season, and everything appeared constantly mutable. They were enclosed, like the arias of a melodrama, and were thus considered to be restful for the soul.

They were not to be questioned or to be disturbed, in contrast with what convention dictated that man should do in relation to mountains and the oceans.

As the great families fell into decadence, some well known residences were turned into luxury Hotels, open to the less aristocratic but more prosperous classes. Later even the Great Hotels had to lower their sights, as it were, and become accessible not only to the big industrialists, to actors and actresses, to passing statesmen and to film stars, but also to tourist groups favoured by foreign exchange rates.

The upper Lake of Como

Majestically set between mountain ranges to the point of being closed under the peak of the snow capped Mesolcina, the upper lake presents a superb spectacle of panoramic vastness which extends to Bellagio and the Lecco branch in the south. However, this is not the only point of interest of the upper lake where we can find art, above all at Gravedona but surprisingly, also in tiny villages lost in the mountains.

In the southern part of **Gravedona**, a few yards from the lake shore, there stand the two oldest sacred edifices: the parish church of St. Vincenzo and the church of St.Maria del Tiglio. St. Vincenzo represents the baroque restoration of a Romanesque church built on the same site as a primitive early Christian chapel of the V century. A few steps away is the **church of St. Maria del Tiglio** - a singular edifice of the region - which originally was the Gravedona baptistry (fifth century) and one still sees inside, fragments of the mosaic (fifth century) which covered the early Christian paving in the form of a triapsidal square, the centre of which was sunk to form the font. The Romanesque structure which we see here, in white and grey marble (circa 1150-1175) was a repetition in a longer version of the early

Christian ground plan with a markedly higher front elevation, accentuated by the belfry set in the middle of the hut-shaped façade (a style from further north). We find the belfry again - at intervals from the fourteenth century on - in octagonal form on top of the roof of the façade. On the outside of the church, we find the usual Romanesque decorative motifs with hanging arches supported in groups on piaster strips or semi-columns, and deep splayed windows. The interior grips us with an already Gothic mystical atmosphere: here we can see the marble font and two galleries which open out at the top of the nave. The far apse is curved into three parts; there are fragments of frescoes from the late 13th to the 16th centuries on the walls as well as a severe white Crucifix which hangs over the small alter.

From St. Maria del Tiglio, our tour of Gravedona takes us through the oldest and most picturesque parts of the town, to the Castle district, where the 16th century **Palazzo Gallio** stands and which was built for Cardinal Tolomeo after the remains of the medieval castle had been levelled to the ground. The very large building which crowns the so-called Sasso (Rock) of Gravedona is something between a fortress and a villa with corner defence towers and pleasant three light windows and with a spacious reception hall on two floors.

Domaso

Gravedona
S.Maria del Tiglio
sec.XII

9

Gravedona

*Gravedona
Palazzo Gallio*

The Cistercian Abbey of Piona

The abbey of Piona stands on the edge of a green promontory at the foot of Mount Legnone, in the municipality of Colico and on the eastern bank of the upper lake of Como. This spot, by the presence of a dense growth of chestnut trees, birches, larches and firs, is one of the most pleasant and picturesque of the upper lake with the distant view on the opposite lake shore and its villages rich in history and art like Dongo, Gravedona, Domaso and Gera Lario.

The abbey is inhabited by Cistercian monks of the Casamari congregation.

The church and cloister of Piona were founded by Cluniac monks in the eleventh to thirteenth centuries which represented the period of maximum expansion of the Order which spread in this territory with the priorates of San Pietro in Vallate di Cosio Valtellino (1078), San Giovanni Battista in Vertemate (1084) and San Nicolò di Figina in Oggiono (1107). The monks settled where the oratory stood, built in the seventh century by the bishop of Como, Agrippino (586-620), and dedicated to Santa Giustina. Of the early construction, only the ruins of a small Moltrasio stone apse remain.

The present church was consecrated in 1138 and dedicated to the Madonna in 1154, the temple was also dedicated to San Nicola of Bari, patron saint of sailors. In 1480, the priorate of Piona was given in commendam by Pope Sisto IV until 1798 when the Directory of the Cisalpine Republic abolished the abbeys and priorates. During a pastoral visit to Piona in 1578, the Bishop of Como found the buildings and furnishings in a state of complete abandon, with the roof, ceilings and paving crumbling and ruined. Having become State property in the last century, the abbey was put up for sale, having various owners until 1937 when it was given to the Casmari congregation. In February 1938, the Cistercians sent a small group which undertook the restoration of the cloisters and the church and successfully started their traditional activities.

The church is rectangular, 27.6 metres long, 8 metres wide and 9.5 metres high and faces East according to the traditional scheme of mediaeval Benedictine architecture. The exterior is simple and severe with walls built in local stone. A bronze door, notable work of the sculptor Giuseppe Abram (1982), breaks the façade and is sub-divided into six panels representing episodes in the life of Saint Benedict.

The interior with one nave, is characterized by sober lines, the two side walls in dark stone covered by a wooden ceiling with horizontal beams, create curvilinear movement towards the outside of the central wall. The apse is entirely covered by frescoes, not easy to read because of their poor state of conservation. At the sides, set in panels, two groups of six apostles carry in one hand the scrole of the Scriptures and with the other hand raised on high they acclaim the manifestation of the Lord. The entire work can also be interpreted as portraying the Ascension.

The cloister, built in the thirteenth century and restored in 1965, is one of the most interesting examples of Lombard Romanesque in Northern Italy. In the form of an irregular quadrangle it slopes towards the church in following the contour of the terrain. Its southern side is at a higher level than the other three, imparting a harmonic movement to the whole. The monks' cells are in the galleries of the cloister as well as the library and the communal meeting hall. The frescoes in the cloister, some of which were taken from other parts of the monastery during the 1960s, date on the whole to the first half of the fourth century.

13

Menaggio

Bellagio

left:
- Mandello
- Lecco

right:
Lecco
Mount Resegone

Lakes Garlate,
Olginate
and river Adda

The centre of the lake: on the left the promontory of Bellagio, in the middle the peninsula

unta Balbianello and, in the foreground the ruins of the castle of Vezio (above Varenna).

Villa Monastero
Varenna

Places and Palaces can have histories which may be as unusual as those of man. They can undergo unexpected changes and live through clashing vicissitued. Villas can become fortresses, like Pliny's Tragoedia, and fortresses can become Villas; austere convents can sometimes become luxurious holiday resorts, and splendid residences can be turned into charitable institutions.

Proud stately homes can fall to the level of hotels, open to a paying public, or be transformed into centres of study.

One such place, known all over the world as the seat of meetings of scientists of the highest level, began as a monastery.

In the year 1208, the building now known as the Villa Monastero was erected by the Cistercian Order, originally as a convent for missionaries and dedicated to Saint Mary Magdalene.

It was the Cistercian custom to set up their centres of worship in particularly attractive spots, and almost always near water.

Clairvaux, Aiguevives, Fontfroide are but some examples of this custom. It was thus natural that they should come to the Lake of Como, and select a site in particularly beautiful surroundings on the lakeside.

The Cistercian rule, however, was strict and little was conceded to the «joy of life» beyond the beauty of the countryside surrounding its centres.

In the «Monastero» nuns lived for many centuries in pious obedience, and perhaps still a little afraid of the warlike events which had evicted them from the Isola Comacina, and had obliged them to move to the Eastern shore of the Lario.

But time changes all, even nuns. Many of them who should have been rapt in the contemplation of God, perhaps with the only diversion of an occasional glance at the centre of the lake, turned their thoughts to other subjects. They even reflected that the Saint who was their Patron had not spent her youth exactly in austerity. They were thus tempted to emulate her life in her weaker moments. Towards the middle of the sixteenth century, the notoriety of their deviation became too well known: the good people of Varenna began to whisper among themselves, but their gossip soon spread along the shores of the lake, reached Lecco and thence to Milan. The Monastery of Saint Mary Magdalene was openly spoken of, not as a place dedicated to prayer and penance, but as a «house of lovers». Such a definition can hardly have been appreciated when it reached the ears of one of the strictest prelates that the Church of Milan had ever known, namely the saintly Archbishop of that City, Cardinal Carlo Borromeo.

After he himself had spent his youth in dissipation, this eminent prelate had acquired the habit of living by bread and water, and of hitting mercilessly priests, friars, nuns and religious orders who strayed from their estate.

The Archbishop requested that the «Monastero» be peremptorily dissolved, and the Pope, Pious the Fifth, promptly issued the order that the ancient convent be closed.

The edifice erected on such a beautiful spot thus became vacant.

A nobleman from the nearby Valsassina, Paola Mornico by name, bought it in the year 1569. His son, Lelio, spared no effort to make his father's house even more beautiful, and, as the story goes, «he turned the lake into a garden».

For many years, the Villa bore the name of Leliana, in recognition of the man who had so greatly transformed it.

In the middle of the nineteenth century it was acquired by the Genazzini family whose only claim to fame in its connection was that of leaving it intact. It then passed into the hands of a sister-in-law of Massimo d'Azeglio, a Minister of some renown, a writer and painter, who also had a Villa on the Lak of Como, at Loveno. The new owner of the former convent was of German origin and her surname, before her marriage, was Seufferheld. She spent many happy years in the Villa. Another German later acquired it, and enlarged and embellished it. As in the case of the Villa Carlotta, the Villa Monastero was confiscated by the Italian Government in 1915, upon the outbreak of war with Germany.

As a handsome war prize, the Villa was granted to Marco de Marchi in 1925 who, in turn, entailed it to the Italian Government in 1936, for it to be the Italian Centre of Hydrobiology and Lake Geomorphology.

The Institute placed it at the disposal of the province of Como, as the «Villa Monastero Authority». For some years, now, it has been the venue of meetings of a very high scientific and literary level.

Probably the most distinguished guest who has so far attended courses in Physics was Enrico Fermi, who is here remembered by an epigraph, inevitably in Latin, where such passages are engraved as "atoma volventia", and "arcana naturae primordia", and of the soul, "tot inter rerum mira pacato".

The structure of the Villa has a somewhat complex appearance, but the eclectic style of its interior is not unattractive, especially to those who appreciate the elaborate style known as «Liberty».

But we need to look no further into the structure of the Villa which is now adapted to its present functions. In the garden, we may be fleetingly attracted by the little temples and by the wells which work, more or less. The visitor will be automatically attracted by two of the Villa's main features which have made the Villa Monastero famous throughout the centuries: the Park and the landscape.

From whatever angle one looks at it, the Lake of Como offers views of considerable beauty and satisfaction. From Varenna, however, where the Villa Monastero is situated, the meeting of the three branches of the lake can be seen from a sufficient distance to be appreciated. This view is a glimpse of an entirely new existence. Although it is in complete

harmony with the environment which surrounds it, it seems to capture the Lario, both as it «extends southwards», and where it flows towards Como. It can be seen while welcoming the waters of the Adda and the Mera. Varenna is a village on the widest spot of the Lake, still comparatively untouched by buidings in cement. Even apart from the Villa Monastero, it is well worth a visit.

The Park of the Villa represents a contrast to those of the Villa Carlotta and the Villa Melzi. While those boast azaleas and rhododendrons, in the one of Villa Monastero one finds roses and cinerarias.

There are also the magestic palm-trees, the eucalyptus-trees, the tangerines, the grape-fruits, the bigarades and the rhubarbs; also the famous magnolia which is three hundred years old, the camphor tree, and goodness knows how many other species of tropical flora happily acclimatized, like the Ancient Greeks who found themselves at home on the Lake of Como.

Villa Melzi
Bellagio

When the lawyer Sommariva was assiduosly engrossed in the work of embellishment of the Villa which his wife had passed to him as her dowry, he would cast an occasional glance across the lake with some concern to try to guess the intentions of his rival in the matter of the vanity of construction, the intentions, in fact of the Duke of Lodi, Napoleon's great friend, a Chancellor of Kingdom of Italy, Francesco Melzi d'Eril. Sommariva's worries were not unjustified. Melzi was immensely rich and on the crest of the wave. He was laying out a garden which was not just an improvement of an existing property but the result of an en- tirely new kind of plan, according to the latest fashion, and placed in the hands of Giocondo Albertolli, a real and imaginative architect, of high repute at the time. When he was engaged in the construction of the Villa Melzi, he had already built the Iatter's Palace in Milan.

The Villa Melzi, indeed, adheres strictly to the neoclassical style introduced in the first decades of the eighteenth century and was extended from Palaces to Villas, and became prominent in public buildings. This style is not entirely extinct here and there all over the world where ostentatious monumentalism is wanted.

In its early stages, neo-classicism stood for innovation and a new freedom of expression as opposed to the heavy repetition of the baroque: everything in this world has a beginning and an end.

From the start, the Villa Melzi was adapted to the concept of a house to be lived in, in accordance, of course, with the way of life which was possible for a great gentleman of the era of Napoleon.

The garden was entirely planned and great earth removals were necessary to achieve the desired effect which is often skilfully illusory. To appreciate this, one should carefully study the avenue of plane trees, the small japanese garden and to note the splendid area upon the shore of the Lake, with its trees, statues and little temples. All the resources of the open air have been thought out and a peaceful

walk among the avenues and the flower-beds gives the impression that the Park is much larger than it really is.

Nothing that one would expect in a patrician garden has been omitted.

There is an enclosure which suggests furtive and mysterious encounters, an original Etruscan cinerary urn, a pond with Cupid's statue, a little lake with its water-lilies, an Oriental stone inscription, and a reference to Apollo and Meleager, marble terrace parapets, the family chapel, at the entrance of which there is an inscription which attributes it to Bramante.

The Villa is not a museum, and the fact that it is lived in makes it much more attractive, pleasant and alive than many others.

The interior is almost entirely neo-classical. The walls are decorated in plaster by Albertolli himself who, in this instance, returned to his original craft as a decorator. There are frescos by Giuseppe Bossi, the brightest of the neo-classical painters of Lombardy, ornaments by Alessandro Sanquirico, the famous scene-painter of La Scala, and the celebrated portrait of Napoleon by Appiani.

If the Villa Carlotta is proud of its Canovas, the Villa Melzi can reply with its Rubens and its Van Dyck.

Today, the owners of the Villa Melzi are the Gallarati-Scotti family. The Duke Thomas Gallarati-Scotti was a Diplomat - Ambassador at Madrid and London immediatley after the Second World War - a man of letters, an impressive representative of the Lombardy aristocracy of the old school. At the Villa Melzi he spent a golden and healthy old age.

Distinguished guests of the Villa in the past include Eugène Beauharnais, the .Empress Maria Fedorovna, Francis the First of Austria, the formidable Metternich and the famous Liszt. If the Austrian Prince repaid his hospitality upon the Lario by the repression of the liberal independence movement, and with the fatuous remark he made «Italy is but a geographical expression»... the Master on the other hand remembered his stay with romantic gratitude.

Nowadays one can visit the garden of the Villa Melzi by the simple expedient of the payment of an entrance fee. This will dispel any excessive hopes of spending a week-end there.

Villa Serbelloni
Bellagio

Pliny the Younger, one of the natives of Como shares with Alessandro Volta and Paolo Giovio the honour of sustaining the fame of his native city. Pliny owned two Villas on the Lake, one in an inlet of the Lario which he called Comoedia, and the second on the Bellagio promontory which, with inevitable logic, he named Tragoedia.

It seems to us incredible, today, that the Bellagio promontory should have any form of tragic connotation. But in Pliny's time, the natural background was as yet untamed, there were few inhabitants, and the promontory itself was somewhat rugged. These factors probably prompted the writer to invest his lakeside residences with a cultural description which one might consider a little precious.

After the Roman era Bellagio lost its characteristic of a residential area and assumed strategic and military importance. It was the battle ground of the Vandals against the Goths, and it is said that Theodoric himself built the fortress upon the highground.

It was not overlooked by the Longobards, and Liutprand altered the fortress so as to make it look less harsh and more suitable as a residence, although it continued to remain fortified.

The castle remained more or less unaltered until Galeazzo Visconti, Duke of Milan, ordered its destruction to get rid of outlaws who used it as a refuge. The Duke Ercole Sfondrati rebuilt the tower on the promontory. Destroyed and rebuilt time after time, the Bellagio fortress remained for centuries an observation point and a defensive structure, and messages were sent fnom its tower, by means of flags by day, and fires by night.

The Ghibellines of Tremezzo, Menaggio and Varenna used it as a refuge when pursued by the people of Como.

During the Renaìssance even Bellagio gradually reduced its fortifications.

The young Marquess Stanga, whose family was of proverbially immense wealth, and who was a Minister of Ludovico the Moor, purchased the promontory and built upon it not a fortress but a palace on the exact spot where the Villa Serbelloni now stands.

Many personages, in all walks of life, passed this way, from the Emperor Maximilian to Leonardo da Vinci. But the waters of the Lake by Bellagio were again affected by bloody rivalries in the first decades of the Sixteenth century in the battles between Gian Giacomo Medici and the "regular" forces of the Sforza.

Pio Francesco Sfondrati was eventually granted the shores by the Emperor Charles the Fifth, and he rebuilt the Villa. After losing his wife he felt called upon to become a priest, and one must admit that even in his new calling he did not fail to make good since he became a Cardinal: this was not all, as his son, Nicholas, who also entered the Church, later was elected Pope under the name of Gregory the Fourteenth.

The Villa remained the property of the Sfondrati family until 1788. It then passed to the Serbelloni family who already owned the very fine Villa of Bolvedro. The Serbelloni in their day were the possessors of great riches and power, and the ramifications of their family were very numerous, and of high standing. Apart from their Villa at Bellagio,

their fame is remembered by a circumstance which they themselves could never have foreseen. Giuseppe Parini was engaged as a tutor of the eldest son of Duke Gabrio Serbelloni, and in the midst of this circle he was able to assess its fatuous atmosphere of luxury and to witness the unfair means which the accumulation of great fortunes engenders. In his work «Il Giorno» (The Day), he was able to describe for posterity that society which repelled and fascinated him at the same time. One day he stood up for a girl who was painfully slapped by the Duchess Maria Vittoria. Parini was dismissed on the spot.

During the years of the Remaking of Italy, the Villa was virtually abandoned, and towards the end of the nineteenth century it was turned into a Hotel. The present Grand Hotel, at the foot of the promontory, dates back to the beginning of the present century, while the Villa on the high ground passed from one owner to another.

The Pricess Torre e Tasso lived there until 1959. It then became a centre and venue for cultural meetings of the Rockfeller Foundation of New York.

The centre of the Lake: on the left, the "Isola Comacina" and the "Balbianello Poin

n the opposite shore, "Varenna" and to the right, the Promontory of Bellagio"

Villa Carlotta
Tremezzo

There are people for whom the Lake of Como means the Villa Carlotta, in the same way as some people believe that the Louvre begins and ends with the Gioconda smile.

And yet this famous Villa, as a whole, has no greater architectural merit than many others which overlook the Lario. We must therefore attribute its universal reputation, which we consciously or unconsciously ascribe to any building which transcends its own beauty, to its location in space, and to the relation it bears to its natural setting and environment, to its climate, and to the natural growth which surrounds it. In short, to the relation between nature and artifice which, as in so many places in the world which have become famous, has achieved the maximum degree of perfection and balance.

There is a well known aphorism which says, «God planted the first garden and Cain, the first city». Man, however, has been greatly preoccupied to bring together these two extremes, and has evolved the garden-city and the habitable garden.

On the Lake of Como, between the eighteenth and nineteenth centuries, the experiment has often been sucessful, with the only limitation that only the well-to-do were able to live in the garden.

We have mentioned successive approximations to a point of balance.

The Villa Carlotta, in its history, exemplifies this approximation to the perfection of a residential plan which takes full advantage of its topographical environment, both by the exploitation of its natural surrounding growth and its climate. Its own possibilities having been identified, it has gradually developed them harmoniously and to the full.

The big «C» at the top of the over-ornate entrance gate in the Via Regina must not be thought to be, as it often is, the initial of the name by which the Villa is known, Carlotta. It refers instead to the name of the Clerici Family who built the Villa in the early eighteenth century, and whose most illustrious member, Giorgio, was President of the Senate of Lombardy, a grandee of Spain, and the recipient of many honours.

In 1856, the Villa Carlotta and its Park were given as a splendid wedding present to Charlotte of Nassau upon her marriage to the Prince of Saxe-Meiningen, the family who were its owners until 1915 when the Italian Government confiscated it as a result of the declaration of war against Germany. It was at first considered to turn the Villa Carlotta into a home for war veterans, but Senator Bianchini contrived that it should be transformed into a public museum, now under its own administrative body. The garden was

The Villa was later inherited by Claudia who married Giovanni Battista Sommariva. It is on this account that the name of Villa Sommariva was used, especially in the nineteenth century.

Francesco Melzi d'Eril was in the meantime completing his Villa on the side of the lake where lies Bellagio and which faced the Villa Carlotta. The splendour of this structure was such as to be a constant irritation to Sommariva who was determined to outdo his rival.

originally designed by the Sommarivas according to the Italian style, that is to say according to a traditional symmetrical, highly artificial, plan which subjects even the flowers and shrubs and the course of the water to an overall discipline of ornamental design. In a garden of this kind, the object is to adhere strictly to the original design, and the constant use of the pruning shears ensures that natural growth does not interfere with the elegant shapes of the hedges and the floral arrangements of the flowerbeds.

The Park was originally much smaller than it is now. Successive enlargements were made in the English style, namely according to the idea of blending the garden with the freedom of nature, eliminating all rigid ornamental planning and substituting a well cultivated quantity of landscape forms and effects.

The Park is today almost the same as that set out by the Saxe-Meiningen family.

Inside the Villa, a number of works of art are on display. One of these, is the Cupid and Psyche by Canova. Other works of Canova on display are his Palamedes, his Venere Italica and his Magdalene. There is also the Group of Mars and Venus by Acquisti (1745-1823), and other famous works of art. One should note in particular the Thorwaldsen Frieze depicting the Entry of Alexander the Great into Babylon, and the spectacular Centrepiece for a Table by Giacomo Redaelli which is an unparallelled example of the Neo-Classical taste of table decoration: in this case, diners could help themselves to salt, oil and vinegar from a miniature Roman Forum ! In the Villa one can also see some important pictures of the neo-classical period: the Apotheosis of Napoleon by Appiani and pictures by Hayez. Also, furniture by Maggiolini and tapestries by Audran. There was a time when one could admire the masterpieces of Gaudenzio Ferrari, Luini, Lotto and Van Dyck, a sign of the splendour with which the princely owners of the Villa Carlotta decorated their residence which was, for them, but a secondary home.

The feeling one gets going round the halls of the Villa is the same as that experienced in all uninhabited buildings. One is inclined to make immediately for an open window and to look upon the magnificent view - an increasing desire to get out into the splendid Park. The time of year which the guide-books rightly recommend is that of the flowering of the azaleas and the rhododendrons, cultivated with superlative landscaping skill which enables the eye to appreciate the general effect and enjoy its beauty. This is not only caused by the flowers themselves but also to certain hidden aspects which can barely be seen beyound the screens of tree and herbacious border.

If the Italian garden represents the ultimate of artifice over nature, the English style stands for the wit of man within nature and the triumph over artificiality. Everything appears entirely natural, but there is not a branch, a slope, a flowering hedge that is not planned to produce a well calculated effect. Upon the range of vivid red, rose and violet colours which abound in springtime there suddenly appear white screens and deep patches of bright yellow which revive a theme: inevitably one is reminded of music, since the theme has no story, nor does it seek to imitate the preoccupations of life. No one here may ask, as is so often asked of a picture, «What does it mean?». There is nothing to discover or investigate: what the eye sees is entirely satisfying and no explanation is called for. It is perhaps the illusion of eternity which the West has always shunned as an obstacle to the «sense of duty»: from the gardens of Eden, of Circe, of Armida and of Klingsor, where Adam and Eve fell, and where Ulysses, Rinaldo, and Parsifal almost succumbed.

It may be difficult today for man to find himself in such famous situations, but we can instinctively feel that there exists indeed something which is strange and mystifying. The possibility that all may suddenly disappear is the special fear of those whom society has chosen to deal in shadows and illusions, namely the poets.

Longfellow for instance, when at Tremezzo, wrote "By Sommariva's garden gate", and even he wondered, "And what if it were all a dream?".

I ask myself, "Is this a dream?
Will it all vanish into air?
Is there a land of such supreme
And perfect beauty anywhere?"

Because beauty is a burden, uncomfortable as truth and as difficult as love. The only escape from this magic of nature is perhaps the experience which many have had of looking beyond this enchanted confined spot and visualizing an uncultivated plot, a field of wild flowers, altogether different from that which man has evolved and cultivated.

Villa La Collina
Griante

Many famous people in the past aimed for Griante as a resort.

It was, in recent times, rediscovered and appreciated as an ideal place for his holidays by the former German Chancellor, Konrad Adenauer.

In his search for some place in Italy both easily accessible to Germany and suitable as a small Chancery, and available as a place of rest and relaxation, the Chancellor at first selected a place near the city of Como, but this plan had to be abandoned when the owners of a splendid residence politely but firmly declined to leave it.

The Chancellor then directed his search to the Lake of Como, thus following the example of many former celebrities who had sought and found a resting place there. Among those who had done this we would recall Giuseppe Verdi, who composed the greater part of his Opera, «Traviata», while enjoying the hospitality of his pubblisher.

Stendhal, the «Milanese» from Grenoble, visited the Lake of Como more than once, and in his work «Rome, Naples et Florence», extolled the beauties of the area of Tremezzo.

The German Chancellor regularly returned to the Villa La Collina at Griante over a span of more than twenty years. This Villa is situated in the middle of a magnificent Park, and from a high spot it dominates the upper reaches of the Lake and the Bellagio point.

In 1977, the Villa La Collina became the Head-quarters of the Konrad Adenauer Foundation and an Internation Meeting place, in memory of the states-man and in consideration of the historical meetings which were held here, and of the European ideas of Adenauer, De Gasperi and Schumann.

Above Griante the lovely little church of San Martino is to be found. From here the place can be seen where the Lake divides into the two branches, one towards the town of Lecco, the other branch that before reaching Como passes kilometre after kilo-metre of parkland, gardens, inlets and small beeches.

Villa del Balbianello
Lenno

Just above the Isola Comacina, a deep green spur which is surrounded by the so-called «Zocca de l'oli» (the Container of Oil) the tourist who crosses the Lake becomes aware of a narrow peninsula, the beauty of which has been enhanced by some buildings designed in the classical style. This is the «back» of Lavedo, which ends in a small fishing port which is one of the sights most frequently photographed of the Lario. Upon this «back», at the time of the Balbiati family whose name is still that of the principal Villa, the Giovio family also lived. This was a prominent Como family, who sold their Villa at the end of the fifteenth century to Cardinal Tolomeo Gallio. It was later returned, through inheritance, to the Giovios, and was purchased by another prelate, Angelo Maria Durini. Towards the end of the seventeenth century, the property passed to the Lambertenghis and, later to the family of the Arconati Visconti.

It will thus be seen that the keys of this paradise passed through many hands, but the hands which created its splendour were those of the consecrated prelates.

Cardinal Gallio, a native of Como, was an important figure of the Ranaissance, a very powerful Secretary of State under Gregory the Thirteenth. Like all the prelates of his time, he delighted in surrounding himself with luxury. He owned two Palaces in Como, a Villa at Frascati, a Villa at Cernobbio (which later became the Villa d'Este), and a Palace at Gravedona. When the Balbiati land became available, he purchased it and commissioned a famous architect, Pellegrini, to design his new residence on the Lake. It is not certain, however, whether that artist supervised the actual building.

Another prelate emulated Cardinal Gallio in evangelical poverty, namely Cardinal Durini, a man of great prestige, Papal Nuncio at many posts, the most important of which was that of Warsaw.

Cardinal Durini was also possessed of the urge to build but, of his many properties, he preferred the Villas he owned at Monza and at Lavedo.

He addressed himself to the enhancement of the splendour of the last named Villa by adding another building to it, the Balbianello, from which he could view both branches of the lake which he called, in accordance with the prevailing paganism of the humanists of his day, the «mirrors of Diana and Venus».

What did the pious Cardinal see in the mirrors which the two goddesses offered him?

The view which probably pleased him most was that of the Isola Comacina, the only island on the Lake, a spot which was once full of monuments and densely inhabited. The Isola Comacina is sited in the middle of the Lake like some fabulous ship, in a spot where the waters are always smooth and unruffled. Hence its popular name of "Container of Oils". It is also renowned for its olive trees which grow here in rich profusion.

The Isola Comacina is a «must» for those who visit the Lario, and it represents a resting spot after the elaborate lakeside gardens, a pause for the enjoyment of a wilder natural, but still enchanting environment.

But even by looking in the opposite direction, the Cardinal could also feast his eyes upon the view of the Bellagio peninsula, and upon the whole of the centre part of the Lario.

While Angelo Maria Durini was admiring both views, enjoying his well-stocked library and learned conversations - he was a friend of Parini - he heard that the French had reached Piedmont, bearing among other things, most displeasing political and social ideas which might even disturb the quiet serenity of the Container of Oils. He promptly thought of instituting, in 1796, a pilgrimage which is still very fashionable among Italians endowed with great fortunes: a pilgrimage to Switzerland and to its very secretive Banks. History, or gossip, recalls that the Cardinal over-burdened his body with bandages filled with gold, and, on bending down, he suffered a renewed former rupture, with fatal results. His heirs almost immediately sold his property to Count Porro Lambertenghi, who engaged, among others, Silvio Pellico as a tutor of his sons. Many years later, Silvio Pellico, from the harsh Moravian fortress of the Spielberg must have looked back frequently and sorrowfully upon the memory of the amenities of the Baldianello.

La Pliniana
Torno

On the eastern bank of the Lario Lake the tourist will find the most mysterious and disquieting of the lakeside Villas, the Pliniana, desolate and withdrawn, some indeed say gloomy, in the area that surrounds the village of Torno.

The edifice seems to reflect an aura of suspended inaccessibility as though still harbouring the many ghosts which are said to have haunted its first owner, Count Giovanni Anguissola from Piacenza who sought refuge in this spot after taking part in the conspiracy which led to the murder of Pier Luigi Farnese in the Sixteenth Century.

Count Anguissola built here an elegant palace. The design of the three arches which are a feature of the central portico suggest the hand of the Architect Pellegrini or at least a strong influence of that eminent master.

The spot upon which the Villa was erected was already well-known at least since the days of the Plinies, on account of a well from which waters spring at regular intervals. This has been of interest to water experts for centuries and has given rise to picturesque popular tales according to which here is the point of convergence between the clear waters of Lake Como and the muddy underground ripples of the rivers of hell. According to Pliny's record, the "spring has its source in the mountain above and three times a day it rises and falls in volume at regular intervals".

The Villa was visited by many famous people during the golden era of its life. The list of its guests includes almost all the names of those who are known to have done the prescribed cultural pilgrimage in their day: Byron, Foscolo, Stendhal, Liszt and many others besides.

Here Rossini composed his opera Tancredi and it is said that it was the romantic and sad atmosphere of the place that influenced the composer's first real break from the controlled conventions of eighteenth century melodrama, and the injection of fiery flashes of love and war which were later to be a feature of all Italian Opera.

Villa d'Este
Cernobbio

In appearance the Villa d'Este is the same today as it is shown in the old prints of this splendid building, except for the superstructure which was built above it when it was converted into a Hotel. Even its interior, especially its reception rooms, is almost unchanged with its somewhat formal décor and the severe whiteness of its entrance hall.

But a process of continuous change has gone on in the life within this luxury residence, though the hurried visitor may not notice it and may believe that the sumptious consistency of its appointments stand for age-old permanence and continuity.

Where once a magnificent Cardinal lived, where a Queen held a carefree Court, now guests live by paying for the hospitality they enjoy unaware perhaps of the exclusiveness and pomp of their predecessors. Rooms to which Exalted Highnesses granted admission, and in which the dangerous political intrigues of the "Risorgimento" were woven, are now the setting for harmless games of bridge and canasta. In the corridors which once resounded with the prayers of devout prelates, or rang with the ribald gaiety of the eighteenth century, can now be heard the strains of soft and repetitive dance orchestras.

The Villa was built in the second half of the sixteenth century, in accordance with plans drawn up by the architect Pellegrini (or so it is thought), for Tolomeo Gallio, the immensely rich "Cardinal of Como", powerful Secretary of State to Pope Gregory the Thirteenth, a prelate who surely cannot be accused leaving his family without a roof over their heads. The Gallio's in fact owned in the Como area: the great palace which bears their family name and is now a college of some repute, a smaller palace known as that of the "Duke", the Winter residence with name the "Gallia", not far from a pied-à-terre called the "Gallietta", the Villa at Cernobbio which we are now visiting, and yet another extensive palace which overlooks Gravedona.

At the beginning of the eighteenth century the Villa went through a phase of contemplation, where periods spent in it were dedicated to prayer and meditation. The contemplative scene changed abruptly when the soldiery took over, in the person of Count Ruggero Marliani the Commander in Chief of the Austrian forces in the area.

At the beginning of the nineteenth century the Villa and its park were acquired by Marquess Calderara, who bequeathed them to his wife, Vittoria Peluso. With a dowry of such substance the widow found it not at all difficult to secure another and even more distinguished husband, Count Domenico Pino, a General and Minister of Napoleon.

The neo-classical and "Empire" characteristics which the General and Minister of Napoleon so greatly admired were then extended to the interior of the edifice, thus completing the cycle of "revivals" neo-medieval which was such an important feature of the "Romantic" period in architecture and painting. Perhaps only a few visitors to the Villa d'Este these days will associate the famous Este name with the magnificent complex created at Tivoli (near Rome) by another Cardinal of the Este family.

The name of the Villa in fact only goes back to the year 1815, when it was bought by Caroline of Brunswick, first wife of George Frederick, Prince of Wales, and later of King George the Fourth of Great Britain. Caroline believed that she was a descendant of the ancient lords of Ferrara, the Este's, and in this belief she was encouraged by the Abbot Bellini who

described her as the "fairest blossom of the Este family". He was of course referring to the Ferrara family who claimed to have come from no less an ancestor than the mythical Hercules, and whose praises a far greater poet extolled, Ariosto; but it is not uncommon for poets, even the very greatest, to be not averse to resort to the flattery of the great and the powerful. The Villa's name is thus at least questionable. It was adopted to satisfy the ancestor-worshipping whim of Caroline of Brunswick who, comfortably installed upon the Lake of Como, lead a life of leisure and pleasure. Indeed, if we are to believe the gossip of the day, Caroline's behaviour was disgraceful, so that the royal consort was collecting and piecing together from a faithful agent all the tales heard from others.

Whatever the truth may be in this matter, the historical fact is that the rumours of a libertine life served to titillate London society and led to a notorious trial, from which the Princess was acquitted, but which allowed the Prince, when he later became King, to exclude his rightful consort from the Coronation ceremony to the great amazement of the Royal Courts of Europe, and the resentment of the British people who disliked their new King and thus sided with those who hated him.

However, meanwhile Caroline had left the Villa which was sold to the Torlonia who quickly passed it to the Orsini family of Rome.

In 1833, the Villa d'Este became the property of Baron Ippolito Ciani, a very rich and very cultivated patriot, an agent and envoy of Cavour - by the Austrian authorities well known - and for the ensuing thirty years the Villa was the centre of political activity and intrigue in the most turbulent years of Italian history

From the year 1868 the Villa d'Este was the residence of the Empress Fedorowna, the mother of Czar Alexander II. For a brief period it acquired a new lustre as a centre of fashion and high living. In 1873, new owners decided to convert the Villa d'Este into a luxury Hotel, as it still is today, among the most famous in the world.

Villa dell'Olmo
Como

The tourist who comes to Como and casts an eye over the lake is immediately struck by the elegance and size of a large Villa straight across the water. He asks what it is and who owns it.

This is the Villa dell'Olmo, and, like so often with great historical monuments, at the source of its history lies a tale of ecclesiastical property. So, when one looks into the history of this Villa, one finds the hand of Church authority.

The site upon which the Villa Olmo was erected is described by Pliny the Younger as a dense forest of elm trees, from which the Villa took its name. A monastery was built on this spot in the early part of the twelfh century, with its adjoining Church of Santa Maria del Vico, the complex being the work and property of the Umiliati Order, an Order which was later to become known, among other things, for its contribution to spinning and weaving and for its

part in spreading the knowledge of the textile craft. It was also an Order with a high degree of independence in its relation with the established Church Authority. Indeed it was a member of this Order who shot at the Archbishop of Milan when it was known that he was considering to reform the Order.

The Archbishop in question was none other than the fearsome San Carlo Borromeo who did not take at all kindly to being shot at and immediately proceeded to close down the Monastery among the elms and with it the Order of the Umiliati itself. In 1618, the Order of the Minors of Saint Francis da Paola obtained possession of the Monastery and with it of the sizeable estate upon which it was built.

In 1664, Marco Plinio Odescalchi was much taken with the attractive spot and was determined to build upon it. After lengthy negotiations in Rome he succeeded in obtaining a permit to erect a "suburban house" in exchange for considerable land and buildings elsewhere.

The Odescalchi went ahead with their plans, first obtaining the services of the architect Innocenzo Ragazzoni, but had to call in the much better known Simone Casati who managed to put right all the mistakes perpetrated by his predecessor and to erect the main body of the most noble structure which was completed in the year 1789. The side wings, which were immediately much criticized and had later to be pulled down, were added in 1796.

For the opening of such an important demesne, it was justified that an appropriate sumptious inauguration should take place. Napoleon himself was invited in 1797, together with his wife Josepine and his sister Elisa.

In 1882 the Villa Olmo was bought by the Visconti di Modrone and with them the last period of private ownership ended. The Villa is today a public monument.

The Visconti's carried out considerable improvements to their newly acquired property. The side wings which had been added as an afterthought to the main noble structure of the building, and had given rise to much criticism, were pulled down, and the entrance portico was greatly enlarged by the removal of internal ceilings so that it now reaches up to an imposing three floors, giving the square edifice a pleasent synthesis of grandeur and proportion. Like this the Villa Olmo can be seen today from across the Lake. Over the great entrance portal hangs the impressive Visconti coat-of-arms, the well-known snake surmounted by the coronet.

Inside the Villa, the Visconti's built a small theatre. The only horror inflicted upon the interior as a concession to a changing world was the installation of a hydraulic lift inside the small but charming Odescalchi chapel.

In 1927, on the occasion of the Alessandro Volta celebrations, the Villa was opened to the public for the first time as a municipal monument.

Since then it remained a centre for cultural manifestations of the town: concerts, particularly frequent during Como's "Musical Autumn".

In the Italian Garden, well planned and kept in good trim, there were once two very old elm trees, reminiscent of the immense one which lived for centuries and is described in the ancient chronicles.

But they were struck by a thunderstorm.

Now, young elm trees have been planted and are entrusted with the task of waxing strong and becoming worthy successors of their illustrious leafy predecessors, since not only men but trees as well have a tradition to uphold.

Como
Historical Notes

Como is situated at the most southerly end of the western branch of the Lake of Como (Lario): the town is flanked on either side by high hills; on a hill towards the plain the Baradello Castle stands sentinel as if still guarding the town which now spreads out on every side. It comprises an inhabited historic centre stretching, more or less, from the lake to the medieval city walls; in this part are to be found houses and small palaces in 18th-century and neo-classical style, plainly constructed, with austerely-decorated doorways and windows, and with little balconies, many of which are charmingly curved in wrought iron. This is not architecture of intrinsic value for theses on art, but its worth is in the design and layout of the city as a whole. Bordering the lake, towards Borgovico and Geno, and beyond, there are many villas, mostly of the 18th and 19th centuries: some are grandiose and of an elegance which, even in the choice of style, bears the stamp of moderation; only in the interiors is there conceded some show of sumptiousness.

Then, also, there is the ancient and hallowed face of Como - this, indeed, is material for treatises on art - with its few Romanesque churches in a good state of preservation - Sant'Abbondio, San Fedele, San Carpoforo, masterpieces of those Maestri Comacini (Master-builders of Como) who are the pride and glory of all Como's ancient diocese. The general impression given by the city is that of a decorum achieved, rather than displayed, being the reflection of a prosperity rooted in toil. This is true, for the long history of the industrious character of the Comaschi (natives of Como) is based on tradition; this has been shown in the woollen industry (now, however, almost abandoned), in the production of silk or, more generally, of fabrics. Even to-day, not withstanding the many industrial enterprises, the production of silk and fabrics is among the most important and typical of the town.

Founded by the mythical Orobi (of whom nothing is known), Como was most certainly inhabited as from the end of the Bronze Age (about 1000 B.C.). Originally, Como was nothing more than a nucleus of settlements which became progressively numerous to the south and west of the presentday city. Most probably the Gauls arrived before the fifth century B.C., and the Romans took Como in 196 B.C., although only after a long struggle did they finally gain it under Julius Caesar.

Julius Caesar rebuilt the town where it is to-day (Novum Comun), repopulated it with 5000 colonists among whom were 500 Greek nobles (perhaps to them are owed names of some lakeside places), and set it on the road to progress which culminated in the first centuries of the Roman Empire. Already, under Rome, Como was a place of strategic importance because of its position at the end of the lake and for the valleys descending from the Alpine barrier. This importance was enhanced by a road which had been built, perhaps, in the first century - the Via Regin a (Royal Way) - which connected Como with Milan and with the Raetia, by way of the west bank of the lake and Chiavenna.

In the time of Imperial Rome Como, encircled by walls of which the perimeter was only a little less than those of the medieval walls, possessed a forum, baths, theatre, temples, villas and a harbour, whilst artisan and commercial activities flourished.

In the region the martyrs, Fedele and Carpoforo, were champions of Christianity and, later, so were the Bishops Felice and Abbondio (end of fifth century): Como was, therefore, a centre for Christian baptism and, later, a most important diocese. Hitherto, under the yoke of the Ostrogoths of Milan, Como had sided with the Byzantines during the Greek-Gothic war (sixth century) until the Longobards took it.

Under Queen Teodolinda who, it is supposed, built and restored the Via Regia which, possibly, from then onwards was called Via Regina (Queen's Way), a period of revival began, favoured by the munificence of the Longobard kings towards the Church in Como and its Bishop. In the second half of the year 1000 the Commune of Como was formed and was recorded in documents as from 1109. It soon became so flourishing and powerful as to preoccupy Milan and become its target. Rivalry broke out and exploded in a war which lasted ten years - the Ten Years' War - from 1118 to 1127 (commencing with the excuse of the investiture of the Bishop of Como), in which the whole region of the lake took part, ending in the semi-destruction of Como in which the militia of the Commune of the Island of Comacina competed. Barbarossa aided the city to rise again, rebuilding houses and its walls (including the Baradello Castle), and vendicated the injuries perpetrated by first furiously attacking Milan and by then annihilating the Island of Comacina (1169). As from the second half of the year 1100 the town of Como,

now revitalized, prospered, whilst encouraging the woollen industry which had been introduced by the Umiliati Order of friars.

After Frederick II's death (1250) civil wars afflicted the city: the most feared faction leaders were the Ghibelline Rusca (or Rusconi), and the Vitani Guelphs (both, however, sometimes changed colours). Finally, Franchino Rusca became Lord of Como (1311), but only for 24 years: the city was, in fact, sold in 1335 to Azzone Visconti who had the enclosing walls constructed. Under the Visconti family who held Como until 1447 (except for an interval between 1408 and 1416 when it returned to the Rusca family) periods of peaceful industry alternated with others of cruel discord. In 1441 the Swiss took Val Leventina and the Gotthard while a few years later the Venetians, in conflict with the Viscontis, invaded the Brianza, the Valsassina and the central region of the Lake, reaching as far as Torno.

Following the ephemeral Republic of Sant'Abbondio (1447-1450), Francesco Sforza installed the Sforza Signoria in Como also which, despite all, survived until 1535. Up to the time of Ludovic the Moor and, in lesser measure, during the prevalence of the French under Louis XII (15001512), fortune favoured Como's civil and economic growth; however, this was followed by continuous mourning caused by the Spanish-French wars which scourged the life out of the Como people. Additional misfortunes occurred in 1516 when the Swiss took the regions of Locarno, Bellínzona and Lugano from Como.

The Spanish domination (1535-1714) is certainly an unhappy memory: bad government, high taxation, blind greed for wealth and the arrogance of the nobility, idle by tradition, constrained the townspeople and those around the lake to emigrate in great numbers, Only some families who voluntarily exiled themselves found fame and fortune: among these were the Artaria, editors in Vienna and Mainz, the Cotta, editors in Stuttgart and in Augsburg, the Brentano and the Canaris families in Frankfurt. The silk industry, introduced into Como by Sigismondo Boldoni, of Bellano, in 1510, languished; the woollen trade survived only with difficulty.

Once the War of the Spanish Succession ended, the Austrians arrived in Lombardy (1714), and the descending parabola which in the beginning of the 18th century had reached its lowest point began, once more, to rise, in Como also, slowly but surely in all fields of activity, gaining speed in the second half of the 18th century. The silk industry's increased production was extensive at this time. The Napoleonic period (1796-1815) was one of prudence and foresight and the regional, if not the national, conscience was awakened. The resulting prosperity was to be seen in an improved administration, better roads and buildings. The walls were lowered; the city lost its severe, military aspect; other villas were built, adding to those which, in the 18th century, already ornamented the lakesides. With the Restoration (1815-1860), the Austrians returned, and then began that Movement of the Risorgimento which in Como and around the Lake found many courageous supporters: among these were Count Confalonieri, Count Porro Lambertenghi, Giacomo and Alfredo Rezia, Gaspare Rosales and Cesare Cantù. In the explosion of 1848 Como boasted with Milan five heroic days of insurrection (18th 22nd March), which concluded in the city's liberation and the installation of a provisional government led by Tommaso Perti. The Garibaldian epoch experienced

one of its most glorious events with the Battle of San Fermo, at Como (27th May, 1859), during which Captain De Cristoforis was killed. Others from Como fought with Garibaldi's troops in the 1849 Defence of Rome (in which Luciano Manara died), the Expedition of the Thousand, in the Battle of Volturno (in which Giuseppe Sirtori took part), and in the Battle of Mentana (Paolo Carcano),

The Maestri Comacini
(Master-builders of Como)

The greatest pride and glory of Como, in fact of the whole ancient Como diocese (which was very extensive), were the Maestri Comacini. They were recorded by Rotari (7th century) and by Liutprando as "Magistri cummageni" or "cumacini" or "Cummacini" those master-builders and craftsmen who belonged to the artisan corporations of builders and stonecutters employing scaffolding and diverse tools, who worked mostly in the regions of Lake Como (Lario), and Lake Lugano (Ceresio). These corporations were the standard-bearers of a tradition of building, sculpture, painting and decoration which endured more than a millennium, that is until the 18th century and later. This tradition was a distinctive one, particularly in some areas: in the Val d'Intelvi (Maestri Antelamici, then the Intelvesi: building, decoration, stucco, plasterwork); by the Lake of Lugano (Ceresio), (Maestri Campionesi: sculpture and architecture, Maestri Porlezzesi: sculpture), and in the Canton Ticino, near by to Como.

The huge area covered by the Maestri Comacini was incredible: their work is to be found in Russia, Poland, Germany and Austria: in almost all Europe. With regard to their work in Italy, the following names may be recalled: Benedetto Antelami from the Val d'Intelvi; families such as the Todari of Maroggia, the Solari of Carona and of Campione, the Cagini of Bissone, then Domenico Fontana of Melide, Guglielmo della Porta of Porlezza, Baldassare Longhena of Maroggia and Francesco Borromini of Bissone.

A brief tour of the walled town

Short round-tour in the walled town.

In the **Piazza San Fedele**, centre of the walled town, and formerly the "Place of the Corn Market", there are still houses overlooking the Piazza which are suported by pillars and dating back, perhaps, to the 16th century. In this area, at one time, there stood the Baptistery of St. John in Atrio (5th-6th century) which adjoined St. Euphemia (now incorporated in the house facing the church).

Nearby, in Via Natta (No. 12), is a Renaissance palace, formerly owned by the Natta family and probably designed by Pellegrini (late 16th century). The style is severe and restrained, softened only by the ornamentation of busts which decorate the tympani of the central windows.

By following Via Vittorio Emanuele, behind the Church of San Fedele, the Piazza Medaglie d'Oro Comasche is reached where the palace which was once owned by the Giovio family, and the Palazzo Olginati, are situated. Palazzo Giovio now houses the Archaeological Museum of Como which exhibits varied facets of the history and life of the city, with special regard to discoveries made during excavations in the surrounding areas and, above all, at the Ca' Morta (House of the Dead). The material comes mostly from necropolises, referring to the "facies" of Como, of the civilization known as "Golasecca" (dating from about 1000 B.C. up till the Roman occupation); a cerimonial cart is of particular interest (of the 5th century B.C.), partly rebuilt; a bronze sword, a boat found in the lake of Monate (13th-10th century B.C.); a pre-Roman inscription in North-Etruscan alphabet; arms, pots, branched candleholders, variously ornamented, and tomb-stones. The Museum also includes Roman material (a basrelief of the 2nd century B.C., and some busts), also early Christian and Romanesque (amongst the latter is a capital from the Basilica of St. Abbondio), 1 3th-century frescoes of the same style as those in St. Abbondio and a group of paintings by Morazzone.

Continuing along Via Giovio and turning into Via Cantù, there comes into view the splendid, neoclassical building designed by Simone Cantoni, constructed on the former site of the church and convent of the nuns of the Order of St. Cecilia. The eight columns in front of the facade came from a Roman edifice and later made part of the Baptistery of St. John in Atrio, which is now no more.

Via Cantù ends at **the tower of Porta Vittoria**, built at the end of the 12th century; it is the finest of the towers of the city walls and is 40 metres high; it was inaugurated by Henry VI of Swabia in 1192.

By following the street leading to Piazza Vittoria, and turning right into Viale Cattaneo we re-enter the walled city by the Via Volta which is particularly rich in noble palaces of the 18th and 19th centuries. Here we find the Palazzo del Registro (No. 85), designed by Cantoni, the neoclassical house where Alessandro Volta was born (No. 62), the late 16th-century Torriani palace (No. 50), serenely elegant and now the headquarters of the Prefettura (Provincial Administration), while facing it is the restored Odescalchi palace (with 17th-century stucco-work and valuable frescoes by G. Paolo Recchi in its rooms) where, it is thought, Pope Innocence XI was born. The Municipal Library was placed in this set of buildings in 1969. Founded in 1663, and in use in Napoleon's day, it possesses more than 311,000 volumes, many of them of great value. Next comes the Church of St. Eusebius, rebuilt in recent times on the site of a very ancient church (of about the 10th century) of which only the small, wall-statue of St. Abbondio remains. This is to be found outside to the right.

San Carpoforo

The Basilica of St. Carpoforo stands on the eastward slope of the Baradello hill. Of the many Romanesque buildings of Como which have been left more or less intact up to the present century this basilica is the finest, and its history is long and interesting.

St. Carpoforo is contemporary to the great church of St. Euphemia, on the Island of Comacina, of which only vestiges of the perimeter remain. It is also contemporary to other lesser churches in the region of Lake Como such as Santa Maria of Loppia, near Bellagio, Sant'Andrea of Campo, near Lenno, and San Fedelino, by the Lake of Mezzola.

Tradition has it that St. Felice, the first Bishop of Como (4th century), transformed a temple, dedicated to Mercury, into a Christian church. In this church he gathered together Carpoforo's mortal remains and those of his companions, following their martyrdom at the time of the persecution of Christians under the Emperor Diocletian.

About the year 724, the Longobard king, Liutprando, seeing the state of disrepair of the little church, decided to restore it, duly enlarging and endowing it generously.

Archaeological remains uphold the veracity of this story of the church of St. Felice: firstly, the discovery of the underground cell, very close to the church, in which the mutilated dedication (MERC)URIO SACR(UM) predominates; secodly some ancient part of the temple also seem to prove the story of Liutprando's church. These are prior to the definitive construction of the 11th century, while some material, at least, which was again utilized, certainly belonged to the church built by the Longobard king.

The Basilica of St. Carpoforo is characterized by the poverty of the building-material used, by the complete absence of decoration, by the irregular distribution of the supports and the heaviness of the arches, typical of Como's churches built in the first decades of the 11th century. It possesses three naves divided in five irregular parts, sustained by plain columns, and is dominated by an ample, raised choir enclosed by a semi-circular apse.

The lack of a doorway at the front of the church, and a corresponding one in the interior, is a curious feature. The original entrances were placed to allow access to the smaller naves on the west side.

The high tower, giving an impression of both lightness and strength, is built in the grey stone quarried by the lake and recalls St. Abbondio's belfries.

Sant'Abbondio

The Basilica of St. Abbondio stands where once there was the early Christian Church of St. Peter and St. Paul, the city's cathedral till 1013. In that year the church of Santa Maria Maggiore became the cathedral (though later pulled down to provide space for the new Duomo). The Church of Sant'Abbondio which now appears before us was built between 1050 and 1058, and was consecrated by Pope Urbano II in 1095. Formerly, a Benedictine monastery adjoined it and its fine cloister may still be seen. As some of the monks came from north of the Alps it is thought that possibly they had some influence on the church's architectural design which shows some uncertainty of style in its Norman and Burgundian motifs of decoration. The monastery was for many centuries a centre of learning and culture. Notwithstanding the great damage the church suffered over the centuries, the work of restoration undertaken in the 19th century and in 1936 has given back to Sant'Abbondio its original and essential aspect.

Sant'Abbondio is, despite its severe appearance, the Como church which weaves the most binding spell: something unique which unites in us a certain innate worldliness with a mystical element typical of the North. It exhibits an unadorned facade (originally preceded by a narthex) divided in descending sectors indicating the interior division of the naves - a very early example in Italy of this type of division - and a magnificent apse, perhaps of a later date.

This apsidal part is elegantly decorated with small columns crowned by the regular motif of the small arches, including variously decorated and tapered single arches: a superb pattern of a structural and decorative order recurring later in many of Como's Romanesque buildings. The twin belltowers are in the style peculiar to Norman architecture.

The lofty, hieratic interior, with five naves ending in apses, finds its liturgical and spacial exaltation just behind the main Altar in the ample presbytery which is screened by the polygonal, principal apse brilliantly covered with frescoes. These depict Stories of Christ and are dominated by the figures of St. Peter, Our Lady, the Redeemer, St. John the Baptist and St. Paul, on the vault, while the Kings (of David's line) look out from the ornamental ribs.

San Fedele

The Basilica of San Fedele, situated in the middle of the town, in Piazza San Fedele, came into being by the addition of a longitudinal nave (1050-1120) to the pre-existing church which was built on a tripartite plan and was dedicated to St. Euphemia (about the 6th century).

Fedele, a Roman soldier at the court of the Emperor Diocletian in Milan, was discovered to be a Christian and imprisoned. Escaping with others, amongst whom was Carpoforo, he took the road to Como, where Carpoforo and his companions were captured and martyred.

Fedele continued his flight as far as Samòlaco (Sondrio) where he was recaptured and then suffered martyrdom (298 A.D.). A little temple was erected on this spot and is still known to-day as San Fedelino. From here the martyr's remains were solemnly brought to the early Christian church of St. Euphemia which, thereafter, was dedicated to him (964). The great merit of the unknown Romanesque architects was to have found how to unite the two complex structures, the old church (later pulled down and rebuilt to the same design, but amplified) and the new, in one spacial synthesis, well-balanced and sure of style. The church underwent rebuilding and restoration from the 16th century up till the present century, but still faithfully conserves its original aspect. Of particular interest, externally, on the west side facing Piazza San Fedele, is the restored, powerfully-designed campanile; on the outside of the east wall, in Via Vittorio Emanuele, the polygonal cupola, the high apse, decorated with an elegant loggia and the doorway, at the side, adorned with 1 2th-century carving which still exhibits a barbaric force.

The spaciousness of the interior with its three naves and full arches, airy women's gallery and cupola, ends finally, with majestic serenity, in the polygonal, central apse, flanked by smaller apses. Of the many works of art of great interest, we note only these few:

The holy water stoups, originally in the church of St. Euphemia (ambulatories); the few frescoes of the late 14th century and of the early 15th century (left apse and right ambulatory); the 16th-century wall-paintings by a follower of Gaudenzio Ferrari - Marriage of the Virgin - the Nativity - Tidings to the Shepherds - the Epiphany (left apse); the "Chapel of the Crucifix" (right apse), with the stucco-work by Diego and paintings on canvas by Carlo Innocenzo Carloni, two artists from the Val d'Intelvi of the first half of the 18th century, and the 17th-century frescoes on the vault, the "Glory of Paradise", by Isidoro Bianchi, a pupil of Morazzone.

Duomo - The Cathedral

The Duomo of Como is the resulting conclusion of four centuries of work (1396-1770). It is imposing for its size but above all for the harmonic fusion of various styles. It arose in an area which gradually became more spacious following the demolition of part of the Broletto, of the Palazzo Pretorio and of the Church of Santa Maria Maggiore. The Duomo was built around this pre-Romanesque church (the Cathedral as from 1013) which was demolished in 1500.

In documents relating to the administration of Milan Cathedral there is an entry showing that "on the last day of April of the year 1396 those administrators yielded to the requests of the Commune and the citizens of Como, permitting that Lorenzo Spazzi, the celebrated architect superintending the initial building of Milan Cathedral, should go to Como to take over the construction of the Duomo".

During the lengthy period of building two dominant styles emerged which blended well with each other: the late Gothic of the facade and the cruciform foot (first half of the 15th century, beginning of the 16th century) and the Renaissance style of the sides (early Renaissance), and of the exterior apses and interior transept (late Renaissance) which do not in any way conflict with the great Juvarra's cupola (1744).

The superb, marble facade was designed by Fiorino da Bontà, of Como, and executed by Amuzio da Lurago and the Milanese, Luchino Scarabota (with much assistance). Some of the work, mostly of the statues which appear on it, is owed to the Rodari of Maroggia (that is to say, the father, Giovanni, and his sons, Bernardino, Jacopo and Tommaso) among whom Jacopo, and even more so, Tommaso, stand out in importance and to whom are due many of the sculptures, not only of the front, but of the whole Duomo (late 15th century and start of the 16th century). On the facade there may be noted the statues of the two Pliny, in niches, by Tommaso and Jacopo.

The sides of the Duomo, designed by the same Rodari, also include the lateral doorways placed in corresponding position; the more ornate of the two, that on the north side, is the so-named "Porta della Rana" ("Doorway of the Frog"), but of the frog, which has been mutilated, there now remains only an indefinite shape. The apsidal part of the Duomo cost a long period of work: however, the basic plan by Cristoforo Solari (1519) underwent no great modification. In the grandiose interior, the Gothic tension of the cruciform base seems to be calmed in

69

the airiness of the Presbytery and the Choir. There are three naves, separated by ten pillars with ogival arches and cross vaults, with transept and apse forming a triple choir space crowned with a fluted cupola.

Among the works of art we note only the most important:

- nine tapestries of the late 16th century;
- various paintings: by Gaudenzio Ferrari, a **Marriage of the Virgin Mary** (St. Joseph's chapel, left-hand nave); by Bernardino Luini, the Adoration of the Magi (St. Abbondio's chapel right-hand nave) and immediately beside it, **the Pala Raimondi** (St. Jeremy's chapel); by Morazzone, the Standard of St. Abbondio (beneath the organ on the right), a precious work of painting and embroidery, and the **Coronation of the Virgin** (on the vault of the Sacresty to the right), admirable for its delicate tones and tenuous light and shade, encircled by little, festive angelmusicians (1611-1612);

- of the marble sculptures, the 18th-century High Altar and the many works by the Rodari family, among which the excellent Deposition (left-hand nave, before reaching the apse), the polyptych in the Chapel of St. Lucia (right-hand nave), and the backs of the lateral doors;

- among the wood-carvings, those of the master, or masters, of the 15th century, representing a Crucifixion (left-hand apse), and the **polyptych in St. Abbondio's chapel** (right-hand nave), probably carved by a master-craftsman from the North at the start of the 16th century.

Volta Temple

On his death, Alessandro Volta (1745-1827) left a priceless heritage of manuscripts and apparatus, of high importance to science, which constituted the greatest attraction of the Volta Exhibition in Como in 1899. This commemorative Exhibition was destroyed by a fierce fire and the instruments, an invaluable proof of Volta's genius, were mostly lost or only recovered in poor condition. Fortunately, the manuscripts conserved in the Reale Istituto Lombardo di Scienze e Lettere (Royal Intitute of Science and Literature of Lombardy) in Milan were saved from total destruction.

A singular aspect of Volta's scientific research traces its origin to the fact that he was self-taught; he confronted his studies by experimenting with apparatus of a wondrous simplicity, obedient to the imperative demands of his personality which propelled him into immediate understanding of the modality of the phenomina under examination.

In 1765, at the age of twenty-four, in the form of a letter to Padre Beccaria, he published a memorandum in admirable Latin in which he explained his ideas on the behaviour of electrical phenomina, opposing the opinions held by Beccaria. This memorandum was to be followed two years later by another, mostly of an experimental nature, in Latin also.

In the Volta Temple there are demonstrated the most significant stages of the research, and the apparatus Alessandro Volta used to achieve his great inventions:
- Electrophorus (1775);
- Induction action and Capacitor (1778-1782);
- Electrometer (1784-1787);
- Theory of Contact and Pile (1792-1800);
- Inflammable Air and Eudiometer (1776-1790);
- Uniform expansion of air due to heat (1791 1793);
- Steam tension (1795).

In sixteen show-cases, more than 200 mementoes and instruments, some of which were re-made, and copies of momentoes, have been gathered togheter, and these demonstrate well the scientific procedure employed by Volta: to form a conception of a theoretical principle and meditate on it with abstraction, and following numerous, enlightened and conclusive tests these could be experimentally verified and confirmed.

At the time Volta commenced his research, most physicists regarded electrical phenomena as a light past-time or as a subject for fatuous discussions. The field of electrical knowledge was restricted: no progress had been made further than the construction of a modest machine for producing electricity by friction. The conductive and nonconductive materials of electricity were known, and also the method of charging and discharging Leyden jars and glass coated with tinfoil, but knowledge was lacking as to the nature of such phenomena.

Distribuzione esclusiva: F.lli CLERICI - Portichetto di Luisago (Co)
S.S. dei Giovi - Via Risorgimento, 7 - Tel. 031-920097

Copyright © 1985-1993 BRUNNER & C. - Como
Testo: Ville e Giardini - Carlo Ferrario
        I Capolavori d'Arte della città - Sandro Chierichetti
Fotografie di: Discacciati Enrico - Guglielmetti Piero - Lanfranconi Sandro - Publiaerfoto -
               Reposo Renato - Ruggieri Leonardo - Vasconi Antonio - Wyss Franco -
               Comune di Como
Finito di stampare nel mese di giugno 1993